MANIFEST YOUR JOURNEY

A VISION BOOK GUIDEBOOK

Jataun J. Rollins, AM, LCSW
AUTHOR, SPEAKER, EDUCATOR, CEO, & ARTISAN

MANIFEST YOUR JOURNEY
A VISION BOOK GUIDEBOOK

CHICAGO

Copyright © 2023 by Jataun J. Rollins
Softcover ISBN: 978-0-9998379-6-2

All rights reserved. No part of this book may be used, reproduced or transmitted in any form or by any means, electronic or mechanical, including photocopying, recording, or by any information storage and retrieval system, without the written permission of the copyright owner, the author and the publisher of the book, except for the inclusion of brief quotations in a critical article or review, magazine, newspaper or for broadcast.

Jai Jai's Consulting & Publishing Company supports copyright. Copyright fuels creativity, encourages diverse voices, promotes free speech, and creates a vibrant culture.

Thank you for buying an authorized edition of this book and for complying with copyright laws. You are supporting the author and allow Jai Jai's Consulting & Publishing to continue to publish books for every reader.

COVER & BOOK DESIGN BY JATAUN J. ROLLINS
Cover Image: AI image of bell hooks

PRINTED IN THE UNITED STATES OF AMERICA
1st Printing

I dedicate this book to my children, Joelle and Jonathan, who were blessed to accept their purpose early in life shaped by their vision of the passions born in them.

WHAT WE DO

IS MORE IMPORTANT THAN WHAT WE SAY

OR WHAT WE SAY WE BELIEVE.

~BELL HOOKS

GUIDEBOOK CONTENTS

PG 5	ACKNOWLEDGEMENTS
PG 10	WELCOME
PG 11	VISION & PURPOSE

SECTION 1: CULTIVATE THE VISION

PG 13	CHANNEL YOUR YOUNGER SELF ACTIVITIES (15 MIN)
PG 14	YOUR LIFE AND SPIRITUAL JOURNEY ACTIVITIES (90 MIN)
PG 15	LIFE VALUES RANKING ACTIVITY (10 MIN)
PG 16	VALUES & CODES YOU GREW UP WITH ACTIVITY (10 MIN)
PG 17-18	HOW ARE YOU PURPOSED POEM
PG 19	HOW ARE YOU PURPOSED ACTIVITY (10 MIN)
PG 20	IF MY LIFE WAS A THEME SONG ACTIVITY (10 MIN)
PG 21	FAVORITE OR INSPIRING QUOTES ACTIVITY (10 MIN)
PG 22	PASSION MAPPING ACTIVITY (30 MIN)
PG 23	BE INTENTIONAL ACTIVITY (15 MIN)
PG 10	DREAM BIGGER ACTIVITY (30 MIN)
PG 10	IMPOSTER SYNDROME ACTIVITY (15 MIN)
PG 26-28	SELF CARE ACTIVITY (15 MIN)
PG 29	GOALS
PG 30-31	NOTES
PG 32	BOOK OF ACCOUNTABILITY TASK TIMELINE

SECTION 2: CRAFTING THE VISION BOOK

PG 35	VISION BOOK INSTRUCTIONS
PG 36	VISION BOOK MATERIALS LIST
PG 37-40	BOOK DESIGN & IMAGE INSPIRATIONS
PG 41	JATAUN J ROLLINS' OTHER WORKS
PG 42	AUTHOR'S CONTACT INFORMATION

MANIFEST YOUR JOURNEY GUIDEBOOK

WELCOME
MESSAGE

Thank you for trusting me to guide you on your manifestation journey. I started vision booking in 2017; several years later I continue to live with intention creating a life that I envision with fulfillment of my dreams, plans, and wishes. I started from a period of my life when I felt most free to dream without limitations - my childhood.

Since I decided to live with intention, I became published, a self-published award winning author, a doll maker, an artist, a jewelry maker, a grant writer, an *InfluencHer Right* Coach, a spoken word artist, a member of the illustrious Zeta Phi Beta Sorority Incorporated, an international speaker, a delegate for Chicago Sister Cities International Shanghai Exchange, a board member for several organizations, CEO of both an LLC and a 501(c)3.

I am living proof that when you hold yourself accountable with intention, you can accomplish what you desire and/or bring you joy!

Jataun J. Rollins
Licensed Clinical Social Worker

Congratulations! The mere selection of this guidebook means that you are pressing RESET! You have just taken the first step with your purchase of this manual using Vision Booking as a tool to fuel your personal and professional successes.

It starts with unlimited imagination, as if there are no barriers or challenges to fulfill achievement of your goals. The vision book you are about to draft requires a plan and this guidebook is your means to a beautiful beginning. Start wherever you like, just promise that you'll be consistent towards completion.

VISION

Vision is defined as *the ability to think about or plan the future with imagination or wisdom,* according to Oxford Languages.

Merriam-Webster also indicates that it is *a thought, concept, or object formed by the imagination and a manifestation to the senses of something immaterial.*

You have to first see where you want to be and know what you want to do in order to see it come to fruition.

PURPOSE

Expect that you will be charged throughout this vision book guide book to:

Think about what you have been purposed for, essentially, seek an understanding of why you are here and what is your calling.

Take assessment of your skill sets and your passion(s).

Reflect on the most awesome experiences you've had in your lifetime & the exhilaration of the things that give/gave you joy.

Be prepared to set time aside to take care of you by committing to utilize this guidebook to provide you with the tools you need.

SECTION 1
CULTIVATE THE VISION

REMEMBER THE YOUNGER VERSION OF YOU

On this page, you are encouraged to remember yourself at the happiest time of your life in your childhood. *Remember the unfiltered, bold version of you. Describe that child's personality. Reflect on an accomplishment you were proud of when you were young. Write five words how others described you.* Set your phone timer for ten minutes to complete this exercise.

DESCRIBE THE DESIRES OF YOUR YOUNGER SELF.

On this part, you are encouraged to reflect on your dreams and wishes when you were young. Think about what you wanted to be or do when you grew up. Set your phone timer for five minutes to complete this exercise.

MANIFEST YOUR JOURNEY GUIDEBOOK

REMEMBER YOUR STORY

In this section, you are to create a timeline from birth to present day of significant events that happened to you in your lifetime. Write positive & memorable moments above the line. Write adverse experiences below the line. Set your phone timer for sixty minutes to complete this exercise.

 --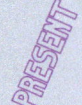

SPIRITUAL JOURNEY ACROSS TIME

In this section, you are encouraged to reflect on your life over time with respect to your practice or experience of Spirituality from birth to today. Use the timeline to chronicle events like, baptism, christening, introduction to religion, when you joined a church (mosque, hall, etc.), when you left the church, singing gospel songs, daily ritual of practice, prayer, meditation, etc. Set your phone timer for thirty minutes to complete this exercise.

 --

MANIFEST YOUR JOURNEY GUIDEBOOK

WHAT HAS THE MOST VALUE TO YOU

Please rank the following values listed below from 1 to 16 based on what you consider to be most important. One means that this is the most important value to you. Sixteen means it has the lowest value of importance to you.
If it does not apply to you mark it as N/A.
For example, if you have no children, you would place N/A next to Parenting.
Set your phone timer for ten minutes.

____ WORK

____ FAMILY

____ HEALTH

____ SAFETY

____ PARENTING

____ CAREGIVING

____ EDUCATION

____ FRIENDSHIP

____ LEGACY BUILDING

____ PEACEFUL LIVING

____ MENTAL WELLNESS

____ PHYSICAL/SELF CARE

____ CIVIC/COMMUNITY LIFE

____ RECREATION/SOCIAL LIFE

____ PROFESSIONAL DEVELOPMENT

____ INTIMATE PARTNER RELATIONSHIIP

____ OTHER _____

VALUES OR THE CODE (S) BY WHICH YOU LIVE

On this page, think back to what the elders or the important people in your life passed on to you as a child, while growing up or even now. Some of things you were told made sense and some didn't. Do you embody those values today? Perhaps you grew up by a code; some people live by the code of the street that might run in alignment or counter to how you were raised.

Write down your values and/or your codes you were given on the left side and write the values that you adopted for yourself. Are they the same, similar but different or completely opposite of your exposure or internalization.
Set your phone timer for ten minutes to complete this exercise.

MANIFEST YOUR JOURNEY GUIDEBOOK

HOW ARE YOU PURPOSED

I want to start this selection beginning with a definition of purpose
and a litany of questions that are intended to spark a thought that leads to action.

Purpose as a noun is defined as the reason for which something is done or created
OR for which something exists - as a verb Purpose is defined to
have as one's intention or objective.

What is THE goal? What is YOUR goal?
Have you begun to construct a plan for the rest of your life?
Have you given a thought to what your purpose is?

Some people are living aimlessly with no idea
or concept of what it means to be purposed,
whether by a higher power, a personal commitment
or to the god that guides them.

So what is your purpose? Why are you here?
How have you imagined your life with intention?
Have you truly lived with intent AND purpose?
How do you define your quality of life?

Is it the clothes that you wear,
the heart that you give, Or the love that you share?
Are you walking and taking up space, not giving back
But just taking up air.

Be thankful for the human experience,
This complex human existence
with all of your faults (as a less than perfect being)
Cascading through this place with humility and grace.

Turn life around and be thankful to be above ground rather than down,
Standing high, full of life and vigor that is being tapped from within
For the new person waiting to be found.

Live with intention everyday,
Rebuke the spirit of procrastination and keep fear at bay.
Live life to the fullest, but ask yourself HOW
Exactly do you define the word full now.

Ask yourself In your quietest moments before make-up and/or hair,
No social media, no one to impress just you sitting there,
Alone with yourself as the focus of interest
Reflect on the life you want and begin to manifest.

How Are You Purposed?

Purpose shifts as it ebbs and it flows
It is you, and you alone who only knows
The scope of your abilities and understanding your why
The whole truth, nothing but the truth and not another damn lie.

Consider the journey of your life as a masterpiece in the making
Are you giving, living or simply just taking?
Are you giving someone else another reason to live another day?
This life is not for the faint, it's not a game or play.

Live is a verb, a call to action
Move beyond fear and self doubt in order to gain traction
Pay attention to the part about living
We need to live, Live in the moment, live in the now,
Live for the days in reflection of how you got over somehow.

You are breathing with some measure of life
Having dealt with the usual and most unusual strife,
Always pushing through and covering errbody, but yo' self.
Let's get your dreams and aspirations off the shelf.

Live in your forgiveness and focus on you
Accept putting you first and believe this is true
The Queen or King is nestled within
Take a leap of faith and let the planning begin

You can live in that body, the one body you have and still not live;
Surrounded with the bones and the memories of the thing or things that you did.

We are counting on you to be strong from the experiences of your past,
Take in the stanzas from the beginning to the last.
Let not these words be in vain
Steeped in a brief, feel good moment only to bring back the pain

Stand up to yourself and challenge you
Go'n and do what you were purposed to do.
You are the only person that can hold back you,
Now tell the truth if I am sitting in your pew.

So I beg the question again, how are you purposed?

JATAUN J. ROLLINS
August 2022

HOW ARE YOU PURPOSED?

On this page, if you are uncertain of your purpose, aren't sure of why you were
created, why you are walking this journey at this appointed time
or you want to break down purpose into its simplest parts
and your reason(s) for existence, this worksheet is for you.
Set your phone timer for ten minutes to complete this exercise.

IF MY LIFE WAS A THEME SONG

On this page, name your favorite songs that give you life; be it soft, slow, Hip Hop, Classical, R & B or Gospel. It could be the songs that got you through heartbreak. Or it could be the songs that get you hyped before going out, on a date, going to church or get you through the day. Essentially, think about which song is more in alignment with you living your best quality of life. Set your phone timer for ten minutes to complete this exercise.

1. List them all here. 2. Reflect on the lyrics that resonate with you the most. 3. Create a playlist of songs that motivate you, so you can use them for setting the mood in completion of this guidebook of activities. Let your songs be a source of your motivation. 4. Consider if any of the lyrics could be the theme for your vision book or something that fuels your energy on the cover of your book.

MANIFEST YOUR JOURNEY GUIDEBOOK

FAVORITE OR INSPIRING QUOTES

On this page, think about some people who have valuable quotes in alignment with your perspective on life. The quotes should be motivational in nature and will complement your book as a method of motivation and encouragement. Place a mark by your top three favorite quotes.

1.

2.

3.

4.

5.

6.

7.

8.

9.

10.

Consider using your quotes for the cover or inside of the pages of your vision book.
Set your phone timer for ten minutes for this activity.

MANIFEST YOUR JOURNEY GUIDEBOOK

PASSION MAPPING

On this page, take a moment to map out your various passions. Think about the activity you absolutely like or love to do or that you can get lost in time working on it. Each circle is for a specific passion you possess. It's the thing when you look up, you don't realize hours have passed. If you have more passions add another circle. Use additional paper, if needed.
Set your phone timer for thirty minutes to complete this exercise.

Expand the details of your passions inside the circle
and the many different directions you envision.

MANIFEST YOU JOURNEY GUIDEBOOK

BE INTENTIONAL

On this page, you are encouraged to thought dump over the various prompts below the various things that you will do to bring your vision to fruition.
Set your phone timer for fifteen minutes to complete this exercise.

I WILL...

BE

DO

GO

SEE

TRY

FACE

STOP

LOOK

BUILD

INVEST

LEARN

TRAVEL

CHANGE

INCREASE

IMPROVE

DREAM BIGGER

On this page, first, dream big about the thing or things you desire to do. Then dream something bigger than that. List it, sketch it or draw your idea (s) as if there were no challenges to you accomplishing it.
Set your phone timer for thirty minutes to complete this exercise.

IMPOSTER SYNDROME, IMPOSTER PHENOMENON, IMPOSTORISM

On this page, it's important that you overstand that even the most, celebrity of celebrities doubt their skill sets, accomplishments or talents with a FEAR turned inward that one might consider one's self to be a fraud. The moment you begin to compare yourself to someone else, you can find yourself spiraling downward.
DON'T DO IT!

Take a few moments to do self-inventory of things or experiences in your lifetime of accomplishments. Beat back the notion that you have not done anything and reflect. Make a list of diplomas, degrees, certificates, awards, honors, great performance reviews, accolades, compliments, and talents.
Set your phone timer for ten minutes to complete this exercise.

SELF CARE AREAS

On these next three pages, take a moment to list the things you would like to address in the respective self care areas you need to work on. Consider starting with areas easiest to begin identifying goals. Set your phone time for thirty minutes for this activity.

PERSONAL

PHYSICAL

ENVIRONMENTAL

PROFESSIONAL

MANIFEST YOUR JOURNEY GUIDEBOOK

SELF CARE AREAS CONTINUED PART TWO

EMOTIONAL

SPIRITUAL

EDUCATIONAL

TRAVEL

SELF CARE AREAS CONTINUED PART THREE

MENTAL

CIVIC

OTHER

Notes:

GOALS

GOALS

NOTES

NOTES

ACCOUNTABILITY TASK TIMELINE

TODAY'S TASKS

TOMORROW'S TASKS

THIRTY DAY TASKS

SIXTY DAY TASKS

NINETY DAY TASKS

SIX MONTH TASKS

ONE YEAR TASKS

I HAVE FALLEN IN LOVE WITH THE IMAGINATION.

AND IF YOU FALL IN LOVE WITH THE IMAGINATION,

YOU UNDERSTAND THAT IT IS A FREE SPIRIT.

IT WILL GO ANYWHERE, AND IT CAN DO ANYTHING.

~ALICE WALKER

SECTION 2
CRAFTING THE VISION BOOK

INSTRUCTIONS

THIS IS THE EXCITING PART!

After putting in all of your hard work in the preceding pages, now you can begin to cultivate your Book of Accountability, you are just about ready to go. Don't concern yourself with whether you are an artist or a creative. Use your imagination and be okay to be free to design as you see fit. It will feel like art class, scrapbooking, organizing and planning all in one. It will even feel therapeutic, that was intentional.

I strategically placed the imposter syndrome activity, if applicable to you, last in Section 1. It is important to look at yourself in a holistic way and not parts of you as an individual. You matter. You are amazing and you have value. When you question your skill sets and talents-----go back to the pages where you have listed your skills and your passions. Don't let imposter syndrome corrupt your mind to think that you are not capable of excelling in life. If someone deems you to be the expert or the one to talk to about something, own it and act accordingly!

Please, do not make one mark in your vision book until you have made progress in the first section where you have begun mapping out your goals and plans to implement what it is that you are about to accomplish.

You can craft your book in portrait or landscape. You can select from the materials list what you envision your book to have; the most important items are a pencil, colored pencils, permanent markers for the covers, modge podge for the book cover to seal the ink, paint brush, scissors, glue or glue stick, and old magazines that you can get from your local library for pennies. Get a nice pen to write in your book.

You can trace images on/in your book, draw, cut images & words from magazines (or print from the internet), create bubble lettering, etc. The way you organize your book can be for the year or any set period of time you desire.

In the areas of self care, you select what you feel you need to work on ensuring that you create a specific task, a time period for completion. You may want to do a book for each of the areas you want to address. The commitment to do one book is enough for me as it is an ongoing process. Keeping up with multiple books and working on them consistently may be cumbersome.

In addition to planned time, work on this book when you have down time, waiting in line, on the bus, riding in the car or when the spirit hits you. You will not finish this book right away. It is a work in progress, just as you are. Take the time you need and operate with intention. Carry your vision book everywhere you go because seeing and touching it will be a constant reminder of the goals you have set inside of your vision book.

Please hashtag #VisionBookwithJai on social media, so that I can see the results of your labor! I get filled when people advance themselves and make accomplishments.

LET'S GET TO WORK!

MANIFEST YOUR JOURNEY GUIDEBOOK

MATERIALS

MATERIAL BASICS

BLANK JOURNAL
PENCILS
COLORED PENCILS
PERMANENT MARKERS
SCISSORS
WASHI TAPE
POST IT TABS
MODGE PODGE
PAINT BRUSH
MAGAZINES

ADDITIONAL MATERIALS

METALLIC MARKERS
ERASABLE PENS
GEL PENS
CORRECTION TAPE
CRAFT KNIFE
PICTURES
STENCILS
STOCK CARD PAPER
HOT GLUE GUN & GLUE STICKS
HEMP STRING OR CORD
COLORED PAPER
STOCK CARD PAPER
GLUE STICK, SPRAY ADHESIVE & GLUE
SKETCHBOOK
ACRYLIC PAINT
STICKERS
OLD GREETING CARDS
MANILA FOLDERS (PLAIN OR DESIGN)
BIBLICAL SCRIPTURES
TAB DIVIDERS
CRAFT FLOWERS
COWRIE SHELLS

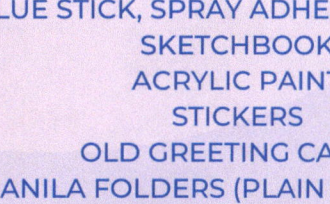

MANIFEST YOUR JOURNEY GUIDEBOOK

BOOK DESIGN & IMAGE INSPIRATIONS

On the next three pages we have provided some representations of ideas, sources of motivation or something you would like to do for your vision book.

You can use these designs as motivating visuals to decorate the inside and outside of the cover of your personalized vision book.

If you are a creative you may want to trace draw or paint what you desire to strive for on your book. Be as free as you want to be in developing your vision book because the only person that it has to make sense to or motivate is you.

Say for example, you desire to lose weight you might apply a scale with the desired weight you want to be, Modge Podge a picture of yourself from when you were your desired weight. Or you could also include a picture of different foods and vegetables that would help you to achieve your goals. Perhaps you could them put the staple items inside of your book under the Physical, Personal or Other box.

MANIFEST YOUR JOURNEY GUIDEBOOK

MANIFEST YOUR JOURNEY GUIDEBOOK

Jataun J. Rollins' Other Works

Manifest Your Justice Journey (2023)

I Don't Wanna Grow Up (2021)
Story Monster Award Winner

I AM COUNTING ON YOU
Activity Book (2021)
Story Monster Award Winner

I AM COUNTING ON YOU
Anti-Stress Coloring Book (2021)

**What's Funny About Dementia?
Laugh to Keep From Crying (2018)**
Royal Dragonfly Award Winner

**UGLY:
Uncovering God's Love for You (2017)**

All of the books can be found on Amazon.

MANIFEST YOUR JOURNEY GUIDEBOOK

JR CONSULTING

CONTACT FOR BOOKS, CONSULTATION, SPEAKING ENGAGEMENTS, VISION BOOK RETREATS, AND VISION BOOK FACILITATION.

 +708.491.3303

 jrconsultinglcsw@gmail.com

 C/O JATAUN J. ROLLINS
P O Box 717 Glenwood, IL 60425

 @Jataun J. Rollins, Therapist

 #VISIONBOOKWITHJAI

MANIFEST YOUR JOURNEY GUIDEBOOK

The author, Jataun J. Rollins, believes wholeheartedly that we are all purposed for something greater than ourselves. it is her hope that you will affirm, embrace and acknowledge the meaning of your life, so that you will make the world in which we live a better place than we will leave it. Ms. Rollins has used these techniques to manifest a vision for herself, believing and saying it out loud in order to hold herself accountable to manifesting her dreams with intention.
NOW SHE IS DREAMING BIGGER!
SPEAK IT OUT LOUD, WRITE IT DOWN, AND MAKE IT PLAIN!

Cover & Book design by
Jataun J. Rollins
Softcover ISBN
978-0-9998379-6-2

www.itsthespiritoflove.com

www.ingramcontent.com/pod-product-compliance
Lightning Source LLC
Chambersburg PA
CBHW041531220426
43672CB00002B/11